My New
School

By Jillian Powell

Photography by Chris Fairclough

Published in paperback in 2014 by Wayland
Copyright © Wayland 2014

Wayland
338 Euston Road
London NW1 3BH

Wayland Australia
Level 17/207 Kent Street
Sydney, NSW 2000

Editor, Wayland: Julia Adams
Produced for Wayland by Discovery Books Ltd
Managing editor: Rachel Tisdale
Project editor: Colleen Ruck
Designer: Ian Winton
Photography: Chris Fairclough
Consultant: Helen Beale (Teacher and Library Coordinator,
Robert Le Kyng Primary School, Swindon)

The author and photographer would like to acknowledge the
following for their help in preparing this book: Aryan and Karan Gohil;
Mr and Mrs Gohil; Headmaster Mr Haselgrove, staff and pupils at
Chad Vale Primary School, Birmingham.

British Library Cataloguing in Publication Data
 Powell, Jillian.
   My new school.
   1. Elementary schools--Pictorial works--Juvenile
   literature. 2. First day of school--Pictorial works--
   Juvenile literature.
   I. Title
   372-dc22

ISBN: 978 0 7502 8285 7

Printed in China
10 9 8 7 6 5 4 3 2 1

Wayland is a division of Hachette Children's Books, an Hachette UK company.
www.hachette.co.uk

Contents

My first day at school

My name is Aryan. Today is my first day at school. Mum walks me to school.

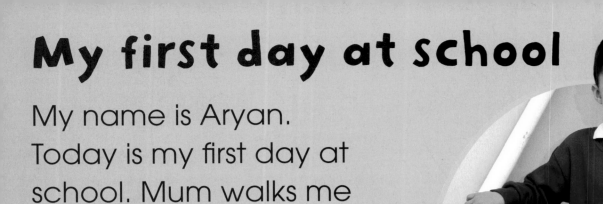

I feel excited and also a bit worried when Mum says goodbye. But Karan comes to meet me.

Karan is in year five. He is my **buddy** at
school. He will show me where everything
is. He shows me to my classroom and tells
me which **peg** is mine.

My class

I am in Reception class. My teacher is called Miss Smith. In the morning she takes the **register**.

I put my hand up when she calls out my name.

After the register has been taken, Miss Smith tells us a story. She asks us questions about the story, too.

Assembly

When we have finished our story, we all go into the school hall for **assembly**.

The **headteacher** says good morning to everyone. His name is Mr Haselgrove.

Mr Haselgrove gives a special welcome to all the new children like me. He tells us he will soon know all of our names and faces.

Paint and play

After assembly, we go back to our classroom. We play with the sand and water.

There are letters hidden in the sand for us to find.

Next we draw with **chalk**.
We make pictures of
fireworks. Miss Millward is
our **teaching assistant**.
She shows me how to
draw a **rocket**.

Snack time

It is break time. I am hungry, so I choose an apple from the school fruit box.

My new friend Sachvir has chosen an apple to eat, too.

Then I go outside to play
in the playground.

Eve and I play with a
hula hoop. It is fun!

Reading and writing

After break time, we learn some new letters. I follow them with my pencil to help me learn their shape and sound.

Miss Smith comes round the class to help us.

Then we play a word game on the **whiteboard**. We take turns tapping the board to answer the questions. I like this game!

Lunch

At lunchtime we sit in the **dining hall** to eat. Some children have a hot lunch.

I brought a packed lunch from home.

After lunch, Karan shows me
how to play basketball. I like
playing with Karan.

Circle time

Next, we sit in a circle for **circle time**.

Miss Smith gets out a special toy tortoise called Timmy. We have to be very quiet for him to come out of his shell. Timmy tells us what the school rules are.

When we have finished circle time, all the children go up to stroke Timmy. He feels very soft.

Going home

It is time to go home already.
Dad has come to pick me
up from school.

I say goodbye to everyone.

I show Dad my
firework picture.
He says that it is
great. I can't
wait to show
it to Mum.

I liked my
first day
at school.

I'm looking forward to
coming back tomorrow.

Glossary

assembly a meeting of the whole school.

buddy an older child who is a friend and helper to younger children at school.

chalk a soft, white or coloured stick that you can use for drawing, often on a blackboard.

circle time a time where the whole class sits together and works as a group.

dining hall a room for eating meals.

headteacher someone who is in charge of the whole school.

hula hoop a hoop that is used for exercise and games.

peg a hook for hanging up clothes.

register a list of the children's names in the class.

rocket a firework that shoots up into the sky, or a machine that can go into space.

teaching assistant someone who works with the teacher.

whiteboard a big board that teachers use to write on and show pictures and words on.

Further information

Books

The Big Day! First Day at School by Nicola Barber (Wayland, 2011)

Where's My Peg? My First Day at School by Jen Green (Wayland, 2007)

My First Time: Starting School by Kate Perry and Jim Pipe (Franklin Watts, 2007)

Websites

www.bbc.co.uk/cbbc/bugbears
This interactive website provides support and advice for children facing new situations, such as 'making friends' and 'finding your way around your new school'.

www.cyh.com
The Kids' Health section of this website includes helpful facts and information on topics such as starting school and changing schools.

www.kidshealth.org/kid/feeling/school/back_to_school.html
This website offers practical guidance on going to school, starting a new school and dealing with problems at school.

Things to do

Speaking and listening
Lets talk! Get into pairs. Think of one question you would like to ask your partner. It could be, 'What is your favourite colour?', 'Do you have any pets?' Then, your partner can ask you a question.

Art
Draw a picture of a face that shows how you felt on your first day at school. For example, it could be a happy face, a sad face or a worried face. You could draw the face on the whiteboard or on a piece of paper.

Writing
Think of a word that would describe the face you have drawn. You can ask your teacher to help you write it down next to your drawing.

Numeracy
Count how many people in your class felt happy, sad or worried. Talk with your friends about the results.

Index